REPUBLICANS

KEEP

WINNING!

i

REPUBLICANS KEEP WINNING!

UNDERSTANDING WHAT VOTERS DESIRE, THEIR FRUSTRATIONS, AND THE REASONS THEY HAVE FOR CHOOSING NOT TO VOTE, AND WHY SOME CHOOSE TO CHANGE THEIR POLITICAL AFFILIATION

P. S. MANN

Percy A. King, Attorney, P.A. 2022

For all the voters who know they deserve better.

TABLE OF CONTENTS

NOTE TO READERS

This book is conversational and written from many different viewpoints. As such, the voice may purposefully change from sentence to sentence. Although the specific viewpoint may be readily discernable at times, I leave it up to you, the reader, to determine who you believe is providing their perspective at any given time

Some words are used interchangeably throughout this book. For example, I used Black and African American, sometimes in the same sentence. This was done for several reasons. First, it was done for simplicity. Secondly, it allows both the reader and individual that may identify with or use one word and not the other to identify the group I am referring to.

I sometimes use conservative interchangeably with Republican. Although all Republicans are not staunch conservatives, as most true conservatives are Republican and many people associate being conservative with the Republican Party, the use is appropriate. It is important to note that I recognize the difference between the two but make general use of the two in this manner because most readers understand the relationship and the use in this concise writing.

Finally, upon speaking to and otherwise researching what was referred to as the lesbian, gay, bisexual, and transgender ("LGBT") community, I discovered that they have now included many more groups and now have added several more letters such that they are in some circles represented as the ("LGBTQQIP2SAA") community. Although explained in a humorous fashion, the book refers to them as "the Alphabet people" for the sake of simplicity.

INTRODUCTION

To get to the point, this book details many of the reasons Republicans have been able to sway voters and win elections in districts where there are many more registered Democrats than Republicans. Importantly, the book explains the real reasons, not the talking points. As many of the reasons are related to the failings of the Democrats, their failings are detailed as well. The importance of understanding why Republicans have been able to win elections cannot be overstated. This book is meant to be a concise articulation of the current political atmosphere, what voters desire, and some of the strengths and weaknesses of the parties that have and continue to determine elections.

As there is no requirement for politicians to be honest with the public, politicians often say what they believe voters want or need to hear for them to identify with the party and turn out to vote for their candidates. Although the truth may resonate with some voters, many others may not believe, understand, or otherwise accept the truth. As such, the truth often gets lost. Many voters are now either frustrated, upset, or otherwise fed up with the political process. Notably, the percentage of voters that are undecided each election appears to have grown, with undecided voters casting the deciding votes in a fair number of elections in recent years. Both the Republicans and Democrats have had their share of success in swaying undecided voters. That registered Democrats outnumber registered Republicans in many states, yet Republicans continue to win elections shows that conservatives have either been able to convince their base to cast their votes in higher numbers than Democrats, or Republicans are doing something right such that they have been able to convince registered Democrats and/or Independents to vote Republican.

With so much misinformation available, voters are looking for information they can trust to help them decide which candidates to support. Even some sophisticated voters are confused and looking for answers. Both parties claim to be religious and to be the best choice for several reasons. Also, each party routinely demonizes the other for one reason or another. The negative claims include: (1) they are racist; (2) they are immoral; (3) they are baby killers; (4) they hate (insert group); (5) they only care about money; (6) they are irresponsible; (7) they want to tell you how to think; (8) they want to take away your guns; (9) they want to take away your right to (insert right); (10) they want to unfairly tax you; and (11) they want to make you like them. What, if any of this is true? There are enough voters looking for the truth and willing to accept it that this book is a necessity.

This book will articulate the thoughts and opinions of several groups of voters and explain why some people have in fact defected from the Democratic Party and voted Republican. I explain some of the rationale that some African Americans, Latinos, and others that have historically voted for Democrats have stated as to why they have or are now willing to vote for a Republican candidate. I also delve into the many other reasons Republicans have been successful and can continue to be successful.

Republicans may use this book to explain to voters why they should cast their vote for conservative candidates. The chapter dedicated to the groups drawn to the Republican Party does a fantastic job of detailing the many reasons African Americans, Latinos, and other long-time Democrats have defected from the Democratic Party. As other voters may have had similar feelings about the failings of the

Democrats, this book will show them that they are not alone in how they feel.

It is likely that some Democrats will not like this book because it shines a light on many of the party's shortcomings. However, ignoring them will not change the fact that the issues discussed have caused voters to be frustrated with the party, not vote in elections, or simply leave the party. As the number of African Americans and Latinos moving up the class scale and earning advanced degrees continues to increase, these same voters now have vastly different concerns, yet the Democrats have not addressed these new concerns because some of them are aligned with conservative ideology, but conflict with their ideology. Democrats will either find a way to address their shortcomings or they will continue to lose ground.

Ultimately, this book was written to provide voters with the information they need to make an informed decision and to provide both parties with vital information regarding some of the issues voters are concerned with and what has swayed them. Politicians create the rules and regulations that the voting public must follow. As such, it is important that they know what voters in fact want and expect from their political leaders

CHAPTER 1
The Three Things That Most Adults Desire, And Using Them To Obtain And Maintain Power And Influence

The first step in determining what people want is to discover why people want things. What is the underlying reason for wanting something… what does this thing they want do for them, and what within them creates this desire? You must understand what the driving force is behind their desires and learn the hierarchy within their value system.

European settlers arrived in North America having been a part of a social class system that controlled how they were perceived by others and their way of life. Having moved to a new country, they were able to create an environment that fostered their self-worth, self-esteem, and self-confidence ("self-wec"). Remember the term self-wec because it will be used throughout this book. Many people use the words self-worth, self-esteem, and self-confidence as if they are interchangeable. However, because they are different, and you can have a great deal of one without the other, they should be distinguished. Leaving that class system behind allowed them to create their own system with them being above the Natives, Mexicans, and the slaves that came later. Although many of the settlers were still considered poor, they discovered that the perception of being superior to others was just as important as in fact being superior to someone else. The perception provided that necessary jolt and support to their self-wec, and it motivated them to support and do anything necessary to maintain their new sense of self.

How a man feels about himself plays a significant role in shaping that man's morals, beliefs, desires, actions, and success. The driving force behind what people value is the need to support and uplift a person's self-wec. Consequently, the most important things to many adults are things that play a significant role in shaping how other people feel about that person, which drives how the people views themselves. The word self may proceed the words worth, esteem, and confidence, but each word is somewhat of a misnomer. Specifically, as all our information regarding how to view ourselves, individual acts, values, likes, dislikes, desires, and sense of import comes from external sources, it follows that a person's self-wec is determined by how others may perceive them and not just from within.

In recent times, the Republican Party has been more successful than Democrats because unlike Democrats, Republicans understand what their constituents and most registered voters value and desire most. While Democrats are busy focusing on what they view are the issues, Republicans focus on determining what a voter values most, what they desire, and what they are willing to accept instead if unable to deliver what voters want. As fear of being viewed in a negative light result in many people failing to be upfront with their true beliefs, historical acts, values, and position on issues, it is imperative that strategies are formulated on fact, not fiction. To be clear, while Democrats proceed based on who voters pretend to be, Republicans base their strategy on who the voters are in fact. The importance of knowing who your target audience is in fact, and what drives them, cannot be overstated.

Generally, successful business owners use the information they obtain about potential customer habits, likes, dislikes, needs, and wants to determine what products to sell and how to sell them to their target customers. First, you must determine the characteristics of your target customers. That is, who is your target customer? Determining what your target customer wants is a particularly important step. However, so is determining if there is a suitable alternative that the target customer will settle for is just as important. The most successful also know how to create customer desire for their product through marketing of thought processes that often results in the target customer not recognizing that the company instilled the desire for the product in them through great marketing.

The marketing of thought processes in politics is akin to a business marketing its product to its target customer. Similarly, you must first determine who your target audience is. Next, you determine what your target audience truly desires. Then, you find out what they are willing to settle for in place of in fact receiving what they truly desire. Although it may sound difficult, it is quite simple. Historically, people in the United States have no issue with voicing their opinions, likes, dislikes, and desires. Also, Americans often subscribe to "group think" and are often willing to follow others they like, are friends with, and those "perceived" to be intelligent, a good person, or wealthy. They do not actually have to be intelligent, a good person, or wealthy. Maintaining the appearance of being one of the three is typically acceptable for many people.

Well, that was quick. I just named the three most important things to most adults instead of beating around the George W. But… did you catch the most important part? Although it is objectively reasonable to assume that most adults would desire to in fact be intelligent, a good person, or wealthy, most care more about how others view them such that it is more important that others view them as intelligent, a good person, or wealthy, than it is to in fact be one of the three.

Subjective intelligence

First, be patient with me. Some of the discussion below may appear to stray off topic, but I promise that it is all necessary to fully address this topic. Although intelligence should be determined on an objective basis, it often is not, thus making it possible for virtually anyone to be subjectively intelligent. Spend a few minutes on social media and you will find a plethora of people obviously with below-average intelligence, who profess to possess the intelligence and/or knowledge of the most talented and accomplished subject-matter expert. There typically will also be many other followers or friends of this person supporting this not-so-genius in their attempt to keep their ignorance and lack of intelligence cloaked.

I have a saying that I use when someone is zealously arguing as if they are correct because they have others who support their position, but they are wrong and truly know nothing about the subject they are attempting to debate. "One of the easiest things to do is to convince an idiot that they are brilliant; however, one of the most difficult things in the world to do is to convince an idiot that well, they are an idiot." I then explain that "as long as you maintain your residency in Idiotville, that you and all of the other residents who believe as you do does not validate said beliefs, nor does it make any of your arguments sound any less ridiculous." What this explains is that just because thousands, millions, or even billions of people are willing to accept some fact, all agree on some point, or "think" the same way does not mean that they are correct or aren't bat-shit crazy. When you are right, do not worry about how many people falsely believe that you are wrong, and they are right. Well, worry if you need to convince them that you are right so that you remain in power or maintain your ability to utilize them for gain.

Okay, back to the desire to have people view you as being intelligent. Isn't it funny that the intelligent people in high school were often shunned, picked on, laughed at, and often not exceedingly popular? Now, a few years later, everyone wants to be perceived as being intelligent. Who knew this would happen? I did. The glamour and prestige associated with achievement in science, math, literature, and politics has a long history that predates the travel to, and subsequent formation of, America by Europeans. The intellectual elite have long been sought after for many reasons. It has been accepted that simply having them at your party, place of business, or just often having them in your presence can change one's status in society. Notably, the ability to state that you were taught by someone revered as being of higher intelligence would raise your status within society. This, notwithstanding whether you retained any knowledge from your experience with that person.

As intelligence is subjective, it is no longer necessary to have actual intelligence to be considered intelligent. There are so many creative ways of convincing someone that they are intelligent, then getting others to either accept the person as being intelligent, or to just go along with it and pretend to view the person as being intelligent. There can be many working parts to pulling off the illusion of intelligence, so keep up.

The first thing you must do is make sure that all the necessary parties are aware of what you are trying to do. As the truly intelligent people will understand, you just need to make sure that you get with the rest of the team and explain their role to them. There are several things that will occur. One of the easiest ways of convincing someone that they are intelligent is creating a history of ignorance and a lack of intelligence in a different or adverse group of people that will be used as a comparator. Whether true or not, evidence that this group is constantly doing, saying, or acting in an ignorant manner and showing a lack of intelligence must be repeated to your target individuals such that they begin to accept it as fact. That this different or adverse group of people may be far more intelligent than described is not important. That the target individuals accept that these negative characteristics can be attributed to the adverse group, resulting in the target group falsely believing that they are better than, and their intelligence is superior to, that of those within the different group is what is important. This truth by repetition is a powerful tool used to convince the intellectually challenged that they are smart. There are many other uses for the truth by repetition method that will be explored throughout this book.

Truth by repetition allows you to create an alternative reality. That may be a reason some of the mischaracterizations associated with creating a false narrative are called alternative facts. Alternative facts allow you to create an alternative reality for the group of people you are targeting. Although fueled by lies, the more each lie about the adverse group is repeated, the more those within the target group gain confidence and become further invested in their position above the adverse group. At some point, providing any evidence or characteristic that makes the target group better than the adverse group is no longer needed. It is simply enough that the target group is not the adverse group because they are stupid, and beneath the target group.

Like comic books, the alternative reality created allows the targeted individuals to maintain a sense of invulnerability, privilege, intelligence, and a false sense of superiority over the adverse group. Although the targeted individuals may not believe that they have superpowers, they often exaggerate their intellect, educational history, knowledge, and analytical ability such that they often create a cartoonish or comic book version of themselves that is insulting to the intelligence of anyone of even average intelligence.

What is average intelligence? Well, most people view average intelligence as what most people have who are not considered to be above average. But what does that mean? Confused? You should be. This view of average intelligence allows everyone to possess intelligence. At best, it creates a situation where most are considered average and there are some outliers with above-average intelligence and some with below-average intelligence. That could not be further from the truth. The most accurate way of explaining the intelligence scale in America is to compare it to the traditional grading scale. Specifically, 90-100 is an A (Excellent), 80-89 is a B (Good), 70-79 is a C (Average), 60-69 is a D (Below Average), and 0-59 is an F (Failing). Based on this criteria, 69.999 percent of Americans have below-average intelligence. Approximately 10% are of average intelligence, while 10% possess above-average intelligence. The final category represents those considered as being of superior intellect, the elite, and geniuses.

As so many Americans have now attended college and graduated with degrees in various fields, we have begun to see that having a college degree is not directly associated with intelligence. Everyone did not put forth the same effort in college, nor did everyone leave college with an "education." It has become painfully obvious that many people crammed, cheated, and plagiarized their way through college. Unfortunately, many people left college with a degree, absent the education. In fact, the education you get from attending a university is causally related to the effort and time you put into your studies while there. Although it is virtually impossible to graduate from college without learning at least something, many people have graduated with master's level degrees that do not qualify as having above-average intelligence.

Being perceived as intelligent is in and lifts a person's self-wec. Those perceived as being intelligent get invited to all the right meetings, gatherings, and important events. They are kept "in the know" on big money-making deals and other important events. If single, there is no shortage of suitors for them. Their opinion on most every subject seems to matter and is sought out. Their position on an issue is rarely incorrect. Their intelligence results in them having little if anything to worry about on a daily basis. Debating against an intelligent person is futile because even when they are wrong, their opinion will still be more correct than yours. Being viewed as intelligent means that you will eventually achieve a level of success that is accompanied by financial success. As intelligent people understand how to invest and make money, their financial success is best described as wealth building. An intelligent person understands the value of being a good person. Consequently, most intelligent people are also good people. Through the need to be perceived as intelligent, I was able to logically connect the desire for wealth and being a good person. Although everyone does not believe that everything I stated is associated with the perception of intelligence, enough people believe at least some of those things, such that it contributes to their desire to be perceived as intelligent.

Bestowing intelligence

The ability to maintain control over people and remain in power is causally related to your ability to **give the people what they want,**

what they are willing to accept instead, or at least your ability to make people believe that they have received what they want. As previously stated, the most successful at maintaining their status have the capability to determine what the people shall want and successfully market, such that people adopt the desires marketed to them as their own.

Intelligent people are the keepers of intelligence. Surprise! Yes, any person perceived as intelligent maintains the ability to bestow the title of intelligent on others. It is as if there is some key that unlocks the cupboard that intelligence is stored in, but it is only accessible by those who already possess intelligence. Although this may seem incredulous, as this way of thinking has historically been accepted, it can be used to provide a false sense of self to those you want as allies, to control, or to keep satisfied. It is not the fault of the intelligent that people think this way or allow themselves to be manipulated. As there will always be those that will utilize such, to have this ability and not use it to your advantage would be wasteful and not consistent with the intelligence you possess.

Now, it is time to explain how Republicans wield the intelligence sword to bestow intelligence… at least the perception thereof. I have already explained how important the perception of intelligence is to adults, so it should be no surprise how easy it is to get most people to accept the gift of intelligence, or that they somehow are intelligent when they have no formal education on a subject, no experience, no real knowledge, and lack the ability to perform an in-depth analysis. None of that matter. People are willing to accept positive characterizations of themselves without any evidence that the characterization is factual.

First, for at least the last two decades, Republicans have marketed on television, radio and recently on social media, that having conservative values and beliefs is associated with intelligence. Specifically, smart people understand that the Republican Party is the best party and will result in a better life for you. This message and similar messages have been repeated by Republicans, such that the truth by repetition phenomenon has taken hold. There has been no shortage of Republicans and professed conservatives appearing on the news, talk shows, podcasts, and other media outlets that zealously tout their background as being one evidencing intelligence, such that everyone should think as they do and join them. They appear clean cut, well spoken, and their points are well rehearsed, resulting in a level of believability that supports their positions. Republicans have successfully created an environment where mere association to the party bestows a perception of intelligence on those that choose to be a part. After all, it is viewed as the smart thing to do.

Additionally, Republicans have historically characterized the Democratic Party as being lazy and lacking in intelligence based on its views and actions. Republican personalities often criticize and make fun of Democrats during their interviews, talk shows, and podcasts. Those stupid, dumb, good-for-nothing Democrats…. This is the message that has been ingrained into many Republican constituents. You dare not be, think like, support, or vote with Democrats because that means you lack intelligence. Once indoctrinated to this extent, it becomes apparent that Republicans cannot agree with Democrats on anything, lest be pulled into Democratic ignorance.

The perceived inability to agree with Democrats on anything results in some Republicans missing out on things that would in fact benefit them. However, as this maintains the cohesiveness of the Republican

Party and the reason the party can keep most of its political figures on the same page, resulting in their ability to get things done, is part of the cost of doing business. Understanding that some soldiers will suffer in battle for the good of the party is something that is part of being a Republican. You will not always get everything that you want, but you will get what you need and more of what you want by being a Republican.

So, now that Republicans have successfully marketed their intelligence in every way possible and explained why joining the party is the only option for intelligent people, it is time to dub thee intelligent. This is done daily on Fox News, Republican podcasts, talk shows, social media, other media outlets, and in homes across America. There is no shortage of Republicans repeating how smart some Republican politician is, or how smart of a decision it was to vote for or against something. You will repeatedly hear what "the smart thing to do" is coming from Republicans. They constantly explain why something they did or supported was wise, and how what the Democrats proposed or did was unwise, and what the potential costs to you will be. They often close with some form of explanation regarding how Republicans are smart for doing, saying, or thinking whatever it may be. This results in the "ah-ha" moment when the Republican watching realizes that intelligence has been bestowed upon them. Their life and status have just been changed. As their views, morals, and beliefs are in line with the intelligent person on television and both are Republicans, notwithstanding their lack of actual intelligence, because they are smart enough to join the Republican Party, they are intelligent. Not only are they now intelligent... at least in their mind, but their association with the Republican Party also makes them somehow smarter than a Democrat with a Ph.D. and decades of expertise on a topic.

The type of constituent just described will maintain their loyalty to a fault. As their sense of self is directly connected to their association with the Republican Party, they will accept almost anything the party does and go along with virtually anything the party supports because it will be viewed as the prudent thing to do. After all, Republican leaders are amongst the most intelligent in existence, so how could this person go against their judgment? They also accept that whatever course of action taken by the party is necessary and proper. Remember, they are proud of their position and happy to be part of a party that perceives them as being intelligent and makes them feel that they play a key role in the party's success and in America's success. To go against the party would be to lose the perception of being intelligent, which is not something worth sacrificing.

The desire to be seen as a good person

Like everything else, whether someone is a "good person" should be viewed under an objective lens. However, what constitutes being a good person is often subjective and the standards for considering oneself a good person often allows most to falsely characterize themselves as a good person. In fact, being a good person requires the absence of many personality traits and character flaws that are common in most people. As such, many people focus on a few acts or beliefs and are willfully blind to the many flaws that should prevent someone from being considered a good person.

Why all the fuss about being a good person? That is a good question. Being perceived or described by others as being a good person directly affects a person's self-wec, lends credibility to a person's actions, suggests that the person is of good moral character, can act as a shield from criticism, and can increase a person's status within a given group.

A good person should have a healthy sense of self-wec. First, part of being a good person is having an internal sense of being worthy and good enough for whatever you desire. Secondly, a good person should not have a problem with self-esteem because they should appreciate and like themselves, have a sense of value, and others should react to them in a manner that supports their self-esteem. Third, good people typically trust their own judgment and qualities. Being perceived as being a good person is an enormous boost to a person's self-wec. Again, the subjective nature of what constitutes being a good person, in conjunction with the subjective aspects of self-wec, makes it easy to see why being perceived as a good person is valued by most adults.

Good people do good things. That is what many would like to believe, or at least pretend to believe. Once someone is characterized as being a good person, their acts are viewed under a different lens. People try to see everything they do as being good if humanly possible. They often must do something inexcusable before their bad act will be seen for what it is. People are willing to take their word and support them without first investigating. It is enough that good ole John Jones said that we all need to do this. If everyone views John Jones as a good man, others will blindly follow him or support him in almost anything he requests their assistance in doing. Having people support you and not question you based on their perception of you is invaluable.

Good people must be of good moral character. Is that not how that goes? Accepting that someone is a good person implies that they are also of good moral character. There is no way that a person can be considered a good person if they are not of good moral character. So, once the title of good person is bestowed upon someone, being of good moral character goes along with it. Morals are standards of behavior and beliefs concerning what is right, wrong, and what is or is not acceptable for a given person. A person's moral principles are driven by a desire to be what constitutes good for them. Being perceived as a good person shows that you have successfully implemented the requisite good moral principles such that you have good moral character. In this case the perception that someone is a good person is accompanied by them also being of good moral character.

Good people rarely try to do terrible things. Even when they do commit bad acts, their status as a good person can act to shield them from criticism or punishment. How many times have you heard of someone making a mistake or purposefully committing a bad act or crime, only to see them get away with it or escape almost unscathed? Conversely, compare that outcome with that of someone viewed as a thug, lazy, or not a good person. The latter will likely suffer severe punishment, while the good person is considered to have made a mistake or had a temporary lapse in judgment. Sometimes simply being a good person entirely excuses behavior that can be construed as bad or immoral. Can a good person be responsible for bad behavior? Alternatively, is it that a good person's behavior is never truly bad? Whatever the case, the perception that you are a good person often changes the criticism or punishment received by the person viewed as a good person.

Amongst a group of people, the person viewed as being a good person enjoys a sense of status that others may not. Others within the group often gravitate to them, have a heightened level of respect for them, and value their opinions regarding many topics. They also are seen as being trustworthy and dependable. The perception that you are a good person instantly gives you credibility and value within your group, and some level of power follows. You just must test it out to see where you stand. With all this in mind, isn't it obvious why someone would desire to be viewed as a good person? Having good-person status can be life changing. The advantages that accompany good-person status are many.

A good person by association

Like the perception of intelligence gained by being a Republican, adopting conservative views and supporting the party, good-person status can be had as well based on such. Republicans are constantly stating how conservative values are better and suggesting that they are good people. It would prove difficult to listen to a Republican elected official speak for five minutes without a mention of how his or her values and principles makes Republicans good people. They often start out with "the good people of" whatever group they represent. Although they may represent a municipality, district, or state that contains both Democrats and Republicans, it soon becomes obvious that the good people reference is directed at the Republicans that he or she represents.

Republicans are so good at convincing others that they are the good guys, that many of their constituents are convinced that everything Democrat is evil and immoral. Republicans do not need to address many issues to achieve the desired "goodness." Simply repeatedly addressing a few hot-button topics as evidencing Republican good and Democratic evil has proven successful. For example, repeatedly blasting Democrats for their position on abortion and homosexuality has allowed Republicans to champion themselves as being morally sound and Democrats as being immoral. Based on those two issues,

Republicans have been able to extend the perception that Republicans are generally of good moral character and Democrats are not. The more alternative lifestyle groups the Democrats add, the easier it gets to evidence Republican morality. Moreover, Republicans have been successful at connecting their values with those of followers of the Christian faith.

Remember how being a good person requires that you also have good moral character? Based on that logic, Democrats cannot be good people because they do not have good moral character. Importantly, Republicans possess good moral character, so it follows that they are good people. Repeating that conservative values are better and make you a good person, in conjunction with repeatedly stating that Democrats are immoral, has resulted in the perception that conservative values are those that every good Christian person should have. This has created a dilemma for some Christians. How can you be a good Christian if you do not have the same morals and values as a Republican? Should your Christian faith be questioned if you decide to no longer support the Republican Party? These are all things that help keep the Republican Party from losing constituents.

Republicans have successfully created an environment where mere association with the party bestows a perception of good personhood on those choosing to adopt conservative values and support Republican choices. By holding themselves out to be good people and associating Republican morals, values, and goals with Christians and other groups perceived to be morally sound, Republicans have basically cornered the good person market. Republicans understand the value of being perceived as a good person.

Republicans have the best shot at gaining wealth

Finally, most adults value what accompanies the perception of having wealth and alternatively, the perception that they have a good chance of becoming wealthy. Money, money, money and more money. The only people not trying to make more money on a regular basis are those that have no money, never had any real money, and those with little chance of ever accumulating any wealth. I mean, why torture yourself by constantly thinking about something you will never have? However, for the rest of us, having money makes the world go around. Even if money cannot buy happiness, it will facilitate a happiness lease, allow you to rent it, or at least put it on layaway. A certain amount of glamour and celebrity also accompanies wealth. People often recognize wealthy individuals due to their appearances in the media or their philanthropic efforts. There is comfort in not having to worry about money. Also, the ability to accumulate wealth implies that the person possesses a high level of intelligence.

People with money often are not required to pay for things. Friends, other business owners, colleagues, and those looking to gain something will often provide complimentary goods and services for the wealthy. These "comps" include, food, clothing, jewels, vehicles, services, and many other items. Why pay for something when it is offered to you for free?

People admire wealth so much that many have been caught pretending to be wealthy in search of fame, money, and the treatment and benefits afforded to the wealthy. Several scam artists have bilked businesses and the rich and wealthy out of millions of dollars during their time pretending to be wealthy. Businesses and the wealthy people they befriended based on their false status provided them with comped goods and services, loans, and paid for things for them under the guise that they, too, were wealthy. Having people believe that you are wealthy when you are not has become so attractive that many have risked going to prison for the chance to live in the shoes of the wealthy, if only for a brief period of time.

Having wealth or at least the ability to accumulate wealth has been associated with members of the Republican Party for quite a while. Along with their goal of fiscal responsibility is the desire to make money and pay as little in taxes as possible, such that you get to keep most of that money. Republicans are generally business oriented and support big business. Republicans are always planning and trying to determine how to create ways of cutting costs and making more profit. Republicans are known for saving money, while Democrats are associated with over-spending.

Republicans cater to the wants and needs of people looking to start a business and create wealth. Republicans are willing to help and support those willing to work hard. If red tape gets in your way, Republicans will spring into action and work with their people in office to help you cut through the red tape. Conversely, Democrats will talk about helping you, but accomplish little, if anything. Republicans will provide you access to many of the people in position to help you succeed.

As most Republicans are not in the habit of bragging about their wealth, although associated therewith, you never know exactly how much a Republican has. He or she may not be in fact wealthy, but their association to the party often implies that they are wealthy or working on being wealthy. There is simply more prestige associated with being a member of the Republican Party.

Republicans have created an environment that fosters self-wec and makes members of the party feel as though they are important.

Republicans are perceived as being serious, loyal, goal oriented, and fixated on making money and being successful. All of this makes it easier for Republicans to lure new voters and those serious about becoming successful in life. Republicans have done their homework. By appealing to the desire to be perceived as being intelligent, a good person, and wealthy, Republicans have been able to persuade a great deal of Americans to join the Republican Party.

CHAPTER 2
Groups Drawn To The
Republican Party And Why

The Republican Party is attractive to several groups of people. It is important to start by explaining the difference between the current Republican Party and the party prior to 1948. And, no, this has nothing to do with the mythological "southern strategy" that so many believe Republicans used to magically convince many southern Democrats, known as "Dixiecrats" to switch parties. I am also not going to delve into a protracted discussion about exactly why the changes to the parties occurred. Instead, as that information is not essential, I will briefly explain it and move on to things that are much more relevant. However, failing to acknowledge that many influential Dixiecrats did switch to the Republican Party, resulting in some of their morals and values being adopted by the Republican Party would be a disservice to America.

Prior to 1948, the Democratic Party maintained dominance in the south. In fact, it was extremely difficult for a candidate running as a Republican in the south to win an election. However, due to Democratic President Harry S. Truman's perceived pro-civil rights platform in 1948, many Dixiecrats walked out. They decided to support a candidate more in line with their values and morals. Consequently, they nominated Strom Thurmond to run as their candidate and held their own convention. Although Truman won the election, this signaled the beginning of the Dixiecrat exodus from the Democratic Party and migration to the Republican Party.

But, still, most Dixiecrats continued to vote for Democratic candidates because they remembered how the south and their families were affected by Republican President Abraham Lincoln and Reconstruction. This changed when Democratic President Lyndon B. Johnson signed the Civil Rights Act of 1964 and the Voting Rights Act of 1965. Almost immediately thereafter, there was a mass exodus of Dixiecrats leaving the Democratic Party for the Republican Party. As many of these new members of the Republican Party were very influential, persuasive, and maintained a rigid set of values, both parties began to change over the next two decades. Candidly, anyone that likens the current Republican Party to the party of Lincoln is either in denial, trying to convince a liberal of Republican greatness, or otherwise using the association to Abraham Lincoln to further a conservative cause.

African Americans

The Republican Party has actively recruited African Americans to join the party. This recruitment is part of the party's attempt to show Americans that the Republican Party is not racist and is willing to include anyone that subscribes to the party's conservative values and ideals. That last part is the most important. Republicans are not seeking to change their agenda, values, strategy, ideals, or course to include African Americans. Any African American seeking to join the Republican Party must be prepared to adopt the conservative platform in its current state and be willing to show the same loyalty to party on all issues that is expected of members of the Republican Party.

Opportunities for African American Republicans

Just what does an African American, or a Black person, depending on how they want to be addressed, get from becoming a Republican? Well, that depends on the person. As the party has made great strides in evidencing inclusivity, great opportunities exist for African Americans to flourish in the name of everything Republican. These opportunities include running for office, employment opportunities, party leadership roles, business and investment opportunities, mentorship, and Democrats' failure to deliver.

African Americans can run for local, state, or national office as a Republican. There are many areas where a Democrat minority candidate has either historically maintained the office, or a minority running as a Republican has a great chance at winning the seat for the party. Republicans are very receptive to the probability of gaining political ground. An African American with the right credentials will have little trouble garnering party support for their effort to gain a seat the party finds advantageous. As such, an African American looking to run for office as a Republican should find an office ripe for the taking, research the incumbent, and determine ways to win the office. Next, create a platform to run on, submit the required paperwork to run for the seat as early as possible, then approach the party about supporting them. Using this structured approach will lessen the probability that the party selects someone else to run for the office that this potential candidate spent considerable time researching and vetting. This unique opportunity has resulted in many little-known Black candidates winning both local and national offices with the backing of the party and the assistance of senior Republicans in office.

African Americans in the Republican Party may enjoy employment opportunities associated with their association to the party. Many members of the Republican Party own businesses. Each of these businesses requires employees to some degree to operate. African Americans active in the party eventually get to know other party members working behind the scenes, at events, meetings, and rallies. This allows the business owners to see that person's values, ethics, and characteristics on a regular basis. Unlike a normal interview where the employer has but a resume, letters of recommendation and a few interview questions to determine if the person is employable, dealing with someone on a regular basis for party business provides a much better picture of what type of employee this person would be. Business owners within the party routinely provide employment opportunities to other members of the party. As many businesses are looking to add diversity to their staff, including in upper management roles, great opportunities exist for African American members of the Republican Party.

By seeking to include African Americans, the Republican Party created a need for African Americans to work for the party. Having other African Americans in positions within the party helping to recruit other African Americans and make them feel welcome is essential to the party's ability to recruit African Americans and dispel the racist mischaracterization of the party. Also, the inclusive direction of the party has resulted in African Americans accepting positions within the party.

Next, most African American Republicans have proved to be extremely valuable and loyal members such that they have been hired in leadership roles. Several African Americans have been selected to lead their local party affiliations. Most notably, an African American was elected as the Republican National Committee Chairman in 2009. Further, like all party members, African Americans can work hard within the party, develop leadership qualities and a following, resulting in opportunities for advancement within the party or the possibility of being selected to run for public office.

As the Republican Party is full of business owners, investors, and people always looking for money-making opportunities, these things are often the topic of discussion no matter what the reason for a gathering of Republicans. Always the right place and the right time best characterizes how most Republicans feel about discussing investment and business opportunities. Making money is important, so why limit the times and places you discuss it? The ability to discuss money-making opportunities with other business owners, investors, intelligent individuals, and like-minded people is why many Republicans are financially set, and are perceived as being wealthy, or as not having to worry about money.

The opportunity of having a prominent Republican as your mentor is invaluable. An African American with a prominent Republican as a mentor would present them endless opportunities for personal, professional, and financial growth. Not only would you learn a wealth of knowledge about virtually everything required to be successful, but you would also have this person's support and recommendation for opportunities that you would not otherwise have access to. Potential employers and business partners would assume that this person had already vetted you and that the mentor vouched for you.

Democrats have failed African Americans

Unlike Republicans, Democrats take their base for granted. African Americans ("Blacks") are the true base of the Democratic Party. Well, Black people and Whites that do not identify as conservative are the base of the Democratic Party. However, for our purposes we will discuss how Democrats use Black voters to win elections only to provide them with little in return.

You do not need to look hard to see that the Democratic Party has largely failed African Americans. Specifically, unemployment rates remain high for Blacks. The poverty rate for Black people remains high. Black males continue to trail other races, and Black women in obtaining a four-year degree. The documented crime rates in predominantly Black neighborhoods remains higher than all others. Legislation designed to effectuate the mass incarceration of Black defendants was passed by Democrats.

The Violent Crime Control and Law Enforcement Act of 1994, often referred to as the Crime Bill, was passed by then President, Bill Clinton, and supported by current President, Joe Biden, who was a United States Senator at the time. Prior to the drafting of the Crime Bill, Republicans had gained political success based on our stance on crime. Specifically, many Democrats believed that H.W. Bush defeated Democrat Michael Dukakis at least partially due to Bush's attack on Dukakis for backing a prison furlough program that resulted in the release of an inmate that went on to commit another violent crime. Clinton and many of the Democrats wanted to gain political capital by adopting an even tougher stance on crime. This resulted in somewhat of a competition between the parties as to which party would prove to be toughest on crime and increase the penalties the most. At the same time, Black leaders were in talks with Clinton and the Democrats about the crime that was plaguing their communities. Democrats spoke with the Congressional Black Caucus, a delegation of Black mayors, and several other Black leaders about the Crime Bill.

Not everyone was on board with the bill. Several prominent Black people stated their objection to the bill and provided context. One such person was Virginia Congressman, Bobby Scott, who voted against the Crime Bill. Congressman Scott explained his position during an episode of "Pod for the Cause," the official podcast of the Leadership Conference on Civil and Human Rights and the Leadership Conference Education Fund. In explaining how he approached analyzing the proposed Crime Bill, the Congressman questioned "[a]re you trying to reduce crime and save money by following the evidence and research, or are you trying to codify a bunch of simple-minded slogans and soundbites to try to help politicians get elected?" He explained that use of the slogans just wastes taxpayer money, does nothing about crime, and increases incarceration to a level of mass incarceration. Additionally, he opined that "regrettably, most of the people, when the dust settled, chose to follow the slogans and soundbites because the evidence that research was clear, this bill wasn't designed for evidence and research, it was just poll-tested slogans and soundbites." Further, Congressman Scott stated that politicians were told that "the Three Strikes You're Out was the number one best vote-getting slogan or soundbite you could blurt out in the '94 election cycle. It'd beat anything you could say about Social Security, health care, the environment." Unfortunately, many, if not most African Americans, are unaware of the extent that Democrats negatively affected their lives and the lives of their families in the name of political capital.

The most insulting thing to many African Americans is that Democratic politicians like Biden and Clinton have continued to blame them for their passage of the Crime Bill simply because they demanded that they do something about the crime that was plaguing their communities. While it is true that African Americans demanded that politicians do something about crime, as violent crime had peaked in many areas of the country, Americans in general were demanding that something be done to curtail crime. Politicians are tasked with protecting the public, which includes protecting citizens from themselves, and their own shortcomings and ignorance. Instead of protecting African Americans, Democrats set them up. They used them as a backdrop to gain political capital with the sections of the bill dedicated to Violence Against Women Act, the ban on assault weapons, and the billions of dollars dedicated to building new prisons that would result in corporate profits.

Democratic leaders are stuck in the early 1960s

Democrats continue to group virtually all African Americans together as if they are all the same, which could not be further from the truth. Democratic leaders are still looking at Black people as if they all are on some level impoverished, under-educated, unable to survive without government assistance, suffer constant unrelenting oppression from Whites and/or the government, and basically view most political issues in a similar manner. Since the sixties, many African Americans have gained wealth, been elected to high government offices, earned advanced degrees from various prestigious universities, moved to the suburbs and gated communities, and adopted political ideologies that vary from that of the Democratic Party.

Gone are the days where even the most well-to-do Black people could not pass on their status to their children. Now, there are numerous African American billionaires that gained their wealth through different areas of business. While many made their money through their association with sports and entertainment, there are those that made their billions through investing, inventions, merchandising, and other types of business ventures. These African Americans are employers and very capable of assuring that their immediate and extended family is taken care of. Also, they generally are not subject to the alleged "oppression" and roadblocks Democrats claim to exist to protect them from. In fact, these people evidence the fruits that come from hard work. Importantly, they do not have the same daily concerns or issues that Black people without means do. Well, at least, many of the issues Democrats associate with most Blacks are not a major concern for wealthy Blacks. Like wealthy people that are White or of any other race, wealthy Black people are often most concerned with taxation, the laws that affect their business, government overreach, and crime. Although a wealthy Black person may experience some form of racism, it will be rare, and often because the person they accused of being racist was unaware of their status and/or who they were at the time. To be clear, their wealth and status can in fact shield them from a great deal of the issues that Blacks without means may face from time to time.

Since the early 1960s, more African Americans than ever have attended and graduated college, with many going on to earn their master's and doctoral degrees. In manufacturing, African Americans complained that young unqualified Whites were unfairly being promoted over them. However, a lot of these young Whites were in fact promoted because they had college degrees. With manufacturing jobs on the decline, many African American families bought into the notion that education was the pathway to a brighter future. Indeed, some African Americans were rewarded for earning degrees relevant to their jobs. As such, there are many more Black people that have raised their status out of poverty into the middle and upper classes. Along with that came positions of power within corporate America and politics for these Blacks. Like wealthy Blacks, they are often able to pass their class on to their children and have political concerns, issues, and ideologies that are not in line with working-class and lower income Black people.

Low-income Blacks often focus their concerns on the minimum wage, the amount of child income tax credit, affordable rental housing, employment laws, health care costs, childcare costs, crime, increased criminal penalties, changes to government aid programs like SNAP, Medicare, and Medicaid, and immigration resulting in workers willing to work for much less than they can afford to accept. Democrats are quick to at least talk about the issues facing poor Blacks. But Democrats fail miserably because many of these issues are shared with poor people in general, but Democrats do not treat them as such. Unfortunately, the few things that Democrats do get passed often have a temporary effect, no real effect at all, or end up putting poor Blacks in a worse position than they were in moving forward.

Democrats have simply failed to deliver

Talk of reparations have been just that, talk only. If Democrats know that they cannot create a plan that this country could afford to address reparations, then they should say so and stop discussing the topic. Democrats know that enough Black people find the topic of reparations, or free money interesting, so they will keep it in their back pocket to parade out whenever they want to galvanize Black people to go out and vote for them. Similarly, most of the issues plaguing the Black community have been handled by Democrats in the same manner, which has been repeated discussion and promises without action to address the important issues they face.

Democrats held the majority in the House and the Senate when Obama was in office, yet they failed to pass most of the legislation they promised their Black constituents. Although Black people have been loyal and the majority have voted solely Democratic dating back to the 1960s, instead of working to help Black people and create laws and opportunities for them, Democrats have focused on other groups such as homosexuals, the other associated sexual orientation groups, women, Latinos, and Asians.

Democrats convinced Black people to include homosexuals and the others with alternative sexual lifestyles in their fight for equality. At first it was just gay males and lesbian females. These two groups adopted two symbols of American joy in the words 'rainbow' and 'gay' such that they transformed them into something else. Now, Jessie Jackson's Rainbow Coalition must be explained to the younger generation, and many people pause when singing the Christmas carol Deck the Halls. Well, is Jesse not telling us something? And does donning gay apparel mean dressing in the clothing of the opposite sex? If that was not bad enough, they have now come for the alphabet. As they add to their constituency, they add additional letters to identify their coalition. It is hard to keep up with…. As of last week, some of them now use the letters LGBTQIA2S+, while some use LGBTQQIP2SAA ("the Alphabet people"). Consequently, I now refer to them as the Alphabet people to make it simple.

As there are numerous Black people that now identify as one of the Alphabet people with families that support them, it wasn't difficult to get many Black people to agree to include them. However, many Black people now feel betrayed. They feel betrayed because they did most of the work to secure civil rights and did most of the time in jail and dying that was associated with gaining these rights. Additionally, some of the Black alphabet people now closely identify as one of the Alphabet people and not as Black. Some do so because they believed that their association results in them being viewed as being somehow better than just being Black, while some do it because they see themselves as having more opportunities if viewed under the rainbow banner. Now, the Alphabet people have said, "Pick me, we have a big following," and the Democrat leadership said, **"OKAY,** we will focus on you now; what do you want?" They asked for everything they wanted. Some African Americans feel the result was that the Alphabet people made more progress in 15 years than African Americans have in 300 years. Importantly, many African Americans believe this lightning-fast progress was due to most of the Alphabet people being of European descent.

Now that the Alphabet people were accepted as allies by Black people, the Democrats began including them in "Diversity" plans that were originally designed to address the failure to include Black people, which at the time was focused on Black men because most jobs were occupied by men then. Once Democrats were able to get corporations to accept that diversity now includes sexual orientation, the flood gates were open. The definition of diversity now includes religion, age, gender, Alphabet people, "minorities," and virtually everything else. As diversity was not meant to effect a total change in corporate boardrooms, working staffs, and management beyond inclusion, this meant that the percentage corporations were willing to commit to diversity would now be up for grabs. Those vying for these diversity positions are Black men, women to include Black women and all other races of women, people of other races and religions, and the Alphabet people, which is mostly comprised of White people. Only a fool would believe that diversity would result in those in power and positions of authority that have made these companies what they are would be replaced without cause just to create the "appearance" of diversity.

Based on diversity as defined by the Democrats, a company can be diverse with no Blacks working there or in management positions because the company employs White women, and other Whites that represent certain relevant letters of the Alphabet. Leave it up to Democrats to create a way to "Diversify" Black people out of the definition of diversity. I have spoken to numerous Black people upset about this, especially Black men. While some Black women have made gains due to diversity initiatives, many Black men have not. This has negatively affected the Black family.

How Democrats continue to convince some Black people that they are their allies when it is their actions that keep Black people in general from excelling is beyond comprehension. Democrats have historically created and continue to create laws and policy proven to harm African Americans. Another example is the national welfare program signed into law by then Democratic President, Franklin D. Roosevelt ("FDR"). The aid to dependent children ("ADC") program included requirements that invited disparate treatment. For example, the mother was required to maintain a "suitable home" for her children, which allowed those case workers tasked with inspecting homes to subjectively determine whether the home was "suitable" or not.

Next, if both parents lived in the home and were considered "able bodied" by the state, they could not receive benefits for sitting around. However, if the man worked his wages would decrease the amount of benefits they qualified for or completely disqualify them. Consequently, many Black families were forced to choose whether to stay together or live apart so that the mother could continue receiving benefits for the children. Initially included was a man-in-the-house rule that disqualified a child from receiving benefits if the child's mother lived with or had an intimate relationship with a man that was not the child's father because he was viewed as a de facto or substitute father. This was so even if the man did not support the child. This was part of the law until the Supreme Court struck it down in 1968. However, the Court's decision clarified that the man-in-the-house rule still applied to "an individual who owed to the child a state-imposed legal duty of support," which means that the child's legal father and any man that the mother was married to. As such, single mothers on government assistance must determine if marrying is in their best interest.

The welfare system has encouraged many Black people to remain impoverished. Children are greatly influenced by their environment and the things they see their parents do. It should not be surprising that a large number of Black females that grew up on welfare followed in their mother's footsteps by becoming single mothers and subsequently receiving public assistance.

In fact, most of the legislation and work Democrats have done that is directed towards Black people is more symbolic than helpful. Insightful Black people have grown frustrated with Democratic inaction and view much of their so-called efforts as insulting to their intelligence. Republicans are different. Republicans do not care what others think of what they do when they have a majority. If legislation is necessary to address the needs of Republican constituents and it is consistent with Republican values and principles, Republicans will act to pass said legislation with or without the advice or support of Democrats. What's right is right, and if it needs to be done, Republicans will work to get it done quickly, and without the need for extended debates.

How many times do Democrats expect to get away with passing legislation or acting in a manner they claim to benefit African Americans, only for it to do much more harm than good? Just how many "Oops" do they get before Black people start referring to Democratic leaders as Britney? Based on how Democrats have failed African Americans, the opportunities presented by Republicans, in conjunction with the needs of African Americans being far from monolithic, political party affiliation has become a personal choice for many African Americans. Democrats do not understand that the days of simply making empty promises of civil rights, equality, and an insulting hand-out in exchange for Black votes are gone. Now, many African Americans have educated and earned themselves into positions where their concerns are more aligned with conservative values. The political choices of these African American voters are based on their morals, what they view as being best suited to reach their goals, and what best suits their personal and familial needs. Consequently, all these things are reasons that numerous African Americans have switched to the Republican Party and many others will likely follow.

Latino conservatives

The number of Hispanic or Latino voters that identify as conservative continues to grow. In speaking to both Latino and Latina voters I discovered that their journey to the Republican Party has been due to a few key reasons. The most important reasons are associated with Latinos being: (1) religious (especially Evangelicals); (2) family oriented; (3) concerned with job availability; and (4) concerned with reducing taxes. Based on these four important topics, Republicans have been able to convince many Latino voters to switch parties, or to vote for them in some elections.

That many Latinos are family oriented and religious, conflicts with the Democrats' stance on abortion, same sex marriage, and

Democratic support for the LGBTQQIP2SAA community ("the Alphabet people"). While many of the Latinos I spoke to were on the fence as to abortion, with some not against it in certain circumstances, it was the support for same-sex marriage, and the type of support the Democratic Party has for the Alphabet people that caused them to sever ties with the Democratic Party. Notably, their concerns were like the concerns that I heard from African Americans and White voters. They reluctantly accepted the Democrats' position when they supported Americans tolerating lesbian and gay men and them being able to sustain employment and doing what they choose in their own homes without fear of retribution. However, simple tolerance was never the goal. Once the Alphabet people gained enough support their true goal was revealed, which was for everyone to accept whatever they do, effect a change in how people view what they do to support such, and for those originally opposed to their lifestyle to become participants therein. In sum, they want the exception to become the norm, and if you do not you will be labeled homophobic, or whatever name they create to negatively describe someone opposed to a member of the grout with the alphabet letter they represent.

Religion is especially important to many Latinos. That Democrats expected to keep Latino voters loyal based on their stance on immigration was a mistake. While some Latinos are concerned with liberal immigration policies, many of the Latinos eligible to vote are not as concerned with immigration because they, nor their loved ones, have pending immigration issues. Also, many of them believe that because they came to America the right way that others should do the same. Some Latinos are tired of illegals perceived as drunks, drug addicts, perpetrators of domestic abuse, and criminals sullying the reputation of Latinos.

Unlike the Black community, there are not as many Latinos that openly identify as gay or as one of the Alphabet people. Consequently, alternative sexual lifestyles and gender identifications are not as accepted in the Latino community. So, this mandate by Democrats to not only accept all sexual orientation, same-sex marriage, fornication, and self-identities, but to condone them even though they conflict with the religious beliefs of Latinos, has caused many Latinos to seek refuge from these far-left ideologies. Democrats are trying to tell voters how to think about personal issues. Even worse, as some of the Alphabet people are caught up in their own delusions of who or what they are, which is subject to change at any moment, Democrats are trying to force voters to participate in these delusions. While some voters of all races may have agreed with allowing people to say or do whatever they want in their own homes, most take issue when they are told that they must accept this and participate therein publicly. Further, that Democrats expect their constituents to publicly condone such and teach their young children that this is acceptable when this does NOT align with their morals, values, and beliefs has turned people away from the Democratic Party.

Gun enthusiasts and Second Amendment rights advocates

The preservation of certain Constitutional and "God-given" rights has often been utilized to refer to the right to bear arms that is *guaranteed* by the Second Amendment of the United States Constitution. Most conservatives treat the right to arm oneself as sacred. Sacred rights do not yield to anything. It matters not how many mass shootings there are, how high crime rates are, or how many accidental shootings occur. The right to bear arms is not tied to the number of incidents where individuals abuse their right. Laws are in place to address those issues. Republicans have fought Democratic encroachment on the right to bear arms for decades. As the text of the Second Amendment lacks limiting language, many gun enthusiasts and virtually all Second Amendment advocates view any attempt at restricting individual gun rights as an impermissible attack on their right to bear arms. As stated in the 2008 U.S. Supreme Court case of *District of Columbia v. Heller,* "Constitutional rights are enshrined with the scope they were understood to have when the people adopted them, whether or not future legislatures or (yes) even future judges think that scope too broad."

Although Second Amendment rights advocates have had some success in advocating for limiting the restrictions courts have allowed to be placed on gun ownership rights, courts have historically upheld many restrictions to our Second Amendment rights. Finding that the Second Amendment right is not unlimited, courts have upheld laws related to the commercial sales of guns, prohibitions on concealed weapons, the possession of firearms by felons and the mentally ill, and carrying guns in sensitive places like schools, hospitals, and government buildings. Notably, in *United States v. Miller,* the Supreme Court held that the sorts of weapons protected are those in common use at the time by the militia. This means that modern, high-capacity weapons like AR-15 style rifles and other large capacity weapons that were not around when the Constitution was drafted are not protected. This is implication by the Court that only weapons available and contemplated at the time are protected. It is this view of the Second Amendment that many gun enthusiasts and most Second Amendment advocates view as flawed.

Liberals cannot be trusted to create the so-called common sense gun control laws they refuse to stop talking about. First, there already are a plethora of laws on the books designed to curb gun violence, yet gun violence still occurs. Democrats have yet to prove that any of the laws they have passed, including a previous ban on assault rifles, have resulted in the decreases in crime that they sought.

Democrats blame the guns instead of the person that impermissibly uses the gun. You would think that many of these mass shootings were due to assault weapons firing themselves instead of it being criminals and disturbed individuals purposefully planning to kill people. Prohibition taught this country that restricting everyone from having does not work. Instead, individuals should be punished for abusing alcohol and committing crimes, not everyone. Prohibition was a massive failure because illegal markets sprung up with no way to keep track of the sales or to assure that the goods were safe for consumption. Similarly, you do not stop people from owning cars because others have hurt or killed people while driving under the influence. You just punish those that get caught driving under the influence.

Criminals will always find a way to get the guns they want. They will get them illegally if they cannot gain access to the guns they want legally. There are more than twenty million people in the United States with a felony conviction. Every year tens of thousands of felons in the U.S. are charged with illegally possessing a weapon. As criminals do not follow the law, please explain how these laws are going to affect the rights of anyone but law-abiding citizens?

Gun enthusiasts know the joy of going to the range and testing out a finely tuned weapon. They know the joy of firing a large caliber weapon at a target resulting in a tight grouping of shots on target. With the increased popularity of AR-15 style rifles, many now enjoy purchasing, customizing, and operating their AR-15 and/or other assault rifles. Further, the sense of safety some get just knowing that they have that for home protection is immeasurable. Moreover, that criminals know that you may have a high-capacity weapon for home security contributes to the decline in break-ins. Criminals do not want any part of meeting up with a homeowner packing a fully loaded AR. Importantly, AR-15 style assault rifles are akin to the weapons our military currently uses and therefore should be protected under the Second Amendment as the kind of weapons a modern "well regulated militia" would use.

Based on the Republican stance on the right to bear arms, voters, historically members of the Democratic Party, have found common ground in our fight to protect our Second Amendment rights. They recognize the fact that instead of trying to pass laws that will actually address the issues they speak of the Democrats are simply toying with the constitutional right to bear arms in an effort to get as many guns off the street as they can. As we have already explained that criminals will always do whatever is necessary to have guns, many gun enthusiasts and Second Amendment advocates do not want to be left defenseless and have joined us in fighting this intrusion.

Lower middle-class and poor Whites

There have been many claims by Democrats regarding how lower middle-class and poor Whites are going against their own best interests by voting Republican. Some Democrats claim that the Republican Party just uses poor and middle-class Whites to maintain power and gives them nothing in return. It sounds like Democrats are confusing their treatment of Black people and all the empty promises Black people have received from their decades of loyalty to the Democratic Party. Like Black Democrats, Whites on the lower end of the financial ladder have received many of the same empty promises regarding job creation, education, and addressing the wealth gap between the poor and wealthy. Democrats have done nothing but talk about these issues instead of helping well deserving lower income White Americans live better lives.

As previously discussed, Democrats do not understand what lower income White Americans desire and value. As such, they cannot provide what is necessary to gain this category of voters' loyalty. Like most people, lower income White Americans desire: (1) to have high self-wec; (2) to be treated as intelligent; (3) to have access to personal and financial growth opportunities; and (4) to be valued. Importantly, Republicans recognize that creating the perception of these things in their constituents works, too. Also, these things can be provided to individuals within the same group in different ways. That is, depending on the individual, the same desire can be satisfied in different ways.

Whites and self-wec

Whites make up the majority in America and are largely credited with having built America. Even if much of the manual labor was provided by Blacks and other minorities, Whites were the architects of what is now the United States and managed its development. The founding fathers of this country were wise White men worthy of the monuments built of them that continue to stand today. Importantly, Whites continue to occupy most of the important positions within the governing body of the United States. Whites came to this country, took it over and persevered. There is no legitimate dispute that this country would not be what it is today had Whites not traveled here from Europe and founded America. Whites fought wars to keep and expand America's borders. Whites are credited with many of the inventions that facilitated America's growth and accumulation of wealth. Under the leadership of Whites, the United States is the most powerful country in the world and is largely viewed as the greatest country on Earth.

Based on all the wonderful things associated with this country that are attributed to Whites, simply being White is a source of pride and a large part of the self-wec of many, if not most Whites.

Every time a Democrat or minority speaks negatively about a founding father, or generally attributes something negative to White people, it is viewed by many Whites as a direct attack or blow to their self-wec. Attacking someone's sense of self often results in that person getting upset and responding angrily, or in a manner that shows that they took what you said personally, notwithstanding whether what you said applies to them. This explains why many whites do not care to hear about slavery, police brutality, the alleged disparate treatment of Black people, so-called White privilege, or how things are so unfair for Blacks. All these things are perceived as personal attacks. It matters not whether the White person listening has participated in any of this personally. They are White and they perceive that you are saying that they are somehow bad, do not deserve what they have, are not a good person, are morally corrupt, and they are not who they think they are. That is a lot to deal with and it often results in the inability for that White person to even continue a conversation about one of those issues. There is often no way that a civil discussion can be had once a White person perceives they are being attacked in that manner.

Republicans understand how Whites feel and how their Whiteness is connected to their sense of self. Republicans operate by creating opportunities for their constituents and thinking of ways to make the lives of their constituents better without attacking their constituents' self-wec. Instead of conjuring up the past and making lower income Whites feel bad about themselves, Republicans support them by making them feel valuable, intelligent, and providing opportunities to advance personally and financially. Republicans support self-wec and are rewarded with loyal members of the party willing to support the party to the end.

The thrill is definitely gone

Blacks and other minorities have been used by Democrats to "guilt" White Americans into supporting laws, initiatives, and other causes that solely benefit those groups. At least for Black people, the guilt was connected to the forefathers of some of these Whites having owned slaves or otherwise participated in some form of oppression toward Black people. Democrats have benefitted from support derived from Whites based on this guilt for decades. Whites that remained in the Republican Party and chose not to support these laws were labeled as racist, insensitive, or bad people, while the Whites that supported these causes were glorified and made to feel good about themselves. For a while, being a Democrat provided a sense of morality to some of these Whites due to their perceiving that they were helping Blacks and other minorities, and therefore being good people. Democrats benefitted from Whites looking to do God's work and help those that could not help themselves and were deserving of help.

That was then! Now, as the Democrats do extraordinarily little, if anything significant to help Blacks, and instead have focused on other groups not enslaved or oppressed by Whites, the guilt that was used to gain their support is no longer motivating these Whites to support the Democrats. Also, that feeling of morality and doing God's work has disappeared. Much of the focus of the Democrats has been on issues involving the Alphabet people, which include same-sex marriage, alternative sexual lifestyles, and gender identifications. As this goes against traditional Christian values and teachings, they are no longer doing God's work. So, White Democrats no longer get to feel good about helping those that deserve it and have lost the feeling of morality associated with their affiliation to the party.

The thrill is gone for many Whites because they are now faced with the revelation that unless they identify as one of the Alphabet people, or have a child that does, they get nothing from voting for a Democrat. In fact, many of them stand to lose by voting for a Democrat. Their taxes will be higher, they will still be made to feel guilty for things they took no part in, and by voting for Democrats they are supporting and approving all the alternative lifestyles that the Democrats support. They are also supporting laws designed to benefit many others over them. They are being asked to fall on a sword and injure or kill themselves with no apparent benefit or purpose beyond someone (the Democrats) telling them that they should do it. Nope, I think not. Based on this nonsense, some Whites are leaving the party with many feeling like an ass for ever joining or voting for the party, with the sentiments of some being: "there's a reason the donkey is used to represent the Democrats."

CHAPTER 3
Donald Trump Has
Been Particularly Useful

Many life-long Republicans were aghast when Donald Trump emerged as the party's candidate for President in 2016. While some feared that the Grand Old Party was being taken over by an extremist faction, others were afraid that the party they worked so hard to shape into the conservative giant it now is would suffer irreparable damage. Also, much to the chagrin of numerous conservatives, many of Trump's supporters openly displayed opinions and attitudes that are best discussed amongst like-minded people, not during a presidential race where liberals can use it to dissuade voters from supporting our candidate. To put it mildly, many Republicans were genuinely concerned about the future of the GOP.

We also remembered that Trump had ties to the Democratic Party and held long-standing relationships with many celebrities and high-ranking democrats. The Democrats made sure to trod out as many old pictures of Trump with the Clintons and celebrity Democrats as the media would allow. In addition, we were entertained by historic videos of Trump with Democrats and making statements thought to present Trump in a negative manner such that traditional Republicans would view him as an outsider looking to either hijack or destroy the GOP. Even if these liberal antics did not work on conservatives, some Democrats hoped that they could sway enough Independents and undecided voters to change the outcome of the 2016 election. Welp, that failed.

It's like Democrats forgot how opposed to Barack Hussein Obama Trump was. Trump stayed in the headlines due to his constant and relentless criticism of Obama's performance as President. Notably, the most memorable were Trump's challenges to Obama's right to be President of the United States due to Trump's belief that Obama was born in Kenya, Africa, and not the United States. Trump's pursuit of Obama's *real* birth certificate helped implant the idea that Obama was an illegitimate president that meant them harm into the minds of many Republicans.

Indoctrinated with the belief that Obama was bad for the country, it was now easy to get our fellow conservatives onboard the anti-Obama train and acquiesce with the Republican plan to vote against virtually every piece of legislation that Obama and the Democrats proposed. As Republicans no longer had to go through the arduous process of explaining to constituents how Obama's…I mean, Democratic proposed legislation was flawed, and/or contrary to the best interests of conservatives, Republicans in Congress simply voted against most of the Bills proposed by Democrats.

We no longer care what others think about our actions

Say what you want about President Trump, but everyone must admit that his style of leadership contains a large amount of "I don't give a damn what you think." Actually, it is more accurately described using the terminology of today's young adults. Specifically, "Trump doesn't give a fuck," or even better, "Trump has zero fucks to give." Trump may ask his followers their desires; however, if they do not fit his agenda, he just tells them that they really want something else that he is prepared to try to give them. Basically, you may think you want that, but this over here is better for you, so hmm, now you want this I am prepared to give you and you are going to love it. It is as if Trump has learned how to use the Jedi mind trick.

Years of being a business owner and the boss of thousands of people looking for him to determine how to proceed and being responsible for telling them what to do has resulted in Trump being accustomed to not being required to consult others before acting, and not having to be concerned with what others think about his actions. Being the boss means exactly that; you are the leader, responsible party, and the final arbiter. Recognizing this quality in Trump, many voters supported Trump based on their belief that he could get many things they wanted accomplished without Trump consulting Democrats, or even caring about Democrats' position on the issue. Further, many Trump supporters relished the thought that Trump would ignore the long-term Republicans in office hesitant to make some of the necessary decisions in fear of how they would be viewed by voters and how these decisions might affect their ability to stay in office.

Trump's fearless attitude towards how others viewed his decisions made making tough decisions much easier. His position that people need to just wait and see how great his decisions will be for them provided the necessary leeway for Trump to move forward without the type of opposition that a President operating without the advice and/or consent of others, the opposing party, and sometimes, his own party would experience. Not only did Trump's followers accept it, most Republicans, Independents, and some Democrats were also on board with giving Trump a chance to prove that his decisions were sound. Although Trump had absolutely no political experience, many Americans were willing to take his word that he was acting in their best interests. Was it because he appeared to be so confident in his abilities and his decisions, or his willingness to go forward without caring about any opposition? Could it be due to the wealth people perceived him to possess? Or was it the promises made and the belief that Trump was their last hope at getting a politician to achieve whatever was on their agenda? The fact that it worked and continues to work is more important than the reason it worked.

For decades Republicans worried about what others thought of their actions, preventing them from getting many laws passed and taking certain steps that would assure that conservative values and principles would be clearly prevalent within the operation and value system of America. Now, armed with the understanding that they can get things done in the same manner Trump did and their constituents and many others will accept it, Republicans can make decisions without worrying about the potential negative consequences associated with their decisions.

Accomplishing things Republicans always wanted

Trump began saying and doing things many Republicans wanted to do prior to being elected President. As a private citizen, Trump gained attention by questioning Obama's country of birth, and thus his ability to hold the office of the President of the United States. Trump's presence on television, radio, and social media was for the purpose of promoting one of his products, a show he was a part of, or to speak negatively about something that President Obama had done or failed to do. Trump was able to go toe to toe with a sitting president as a private citizen while many seasoned politicians failed to even get Obama's attention.

There are several things that Republicans have wanted to accomplish but had never fully accomplished. One of the biggest accomplishments was getting the party to blindly support Republican proposed legislation without the need to conduct protracted discussions and bartering. Under Trump, we continuously saw the party come together to quickly pass vital legislation and to confirm Supreme Court Justices. We discovered that we can accomplish almost anything if we stick together.

The Trump tax bill is viewed by many as one of the most important pieces of Republican legislation ever passed. Republicans did not allow Democrats time to water it down or force any unnecessary discussion. What Democrats were unaware of is that Republicans were prepared for the moment when we could reverse some of the tax hikes Democrats have instituted that stifled business, and economic growth in this country. The law contained tax breaks vital to many businesses and business owners. Those tax breaks encouraged many to bring their money being held in foreign countries back to the United States. Corporations saw a 40% decrease in their tax levy with the decrease from 35% to 21%. The highest individual tax rate was decreased, and business owners with pass-through entities are now able to take advantage of the 20% income shield. Importantly, it simplified taxes for millions of Americans who now take the greatly increased standard deduction instead of itemizing.

Trump was able to minimize America's need for a candidate with political experience. In fact, the need for experience has all but gone out the door and, in some cases, having too much experience can cost you the election. Experience was once deemed necessary because voters wanted to make sure that they could trust that the person in office could handle whatever adversity they faced. Now, unless the incumbent has accomplished most of what they have promised, their experience is viewed negatively. You are perceived as being a career politician or having a track record of failed promises and being someone that cannot be trusted to follow the will of the people. Previously, incumbents were almost assured that they would be reelected when they ran against unknowns or someone with little to no political experience. That is no longer the case.

Although Republicans had focused on the negative aspects of the Democratic Party during elections, Trump took it to a new level and showed Republicans how to be successful. The key to beating a Democratic incumbent includes Republicans selecting a popular candidate with little to no political experience. That candidate must address the issues popular with Republicans and addresses the many deficiencies in Democratic policies, and repeatedly demonize the extreme issues and beliefs of the far left. As many Democrats take issue with some of these issues and beliefs, a Republican candidate that follows this formula has a chance at unseating a Democrat incumbent. Voters must be repeatedly reminded about the negative aspects and consequences associated with the policies of Democrats. It's not enough to just talk about them during debates, voters need constant reminders daily if possible. Voters need to be convinced that the policies and beliefs of the Democrats are so bad that they cannot vote for them under any circumstances. We use the conservative lens to characterize how we view Democrats and their policies such that most of their policies are arguably so bad that no one should ever vote for a Democrat.

Trump was able to convince millions of Americans that the beliefs, and policies associated with the Democrats are so immoral, ungodly, negative, unreasonable, and unsavory that many of them may never vote for a Democrat for the rest of their lives. Millions of Americans have a level of distrust and disdain for Democrats that I do not think ever existed. Now, Republicans have been able to enlighten or otherwise open the eyes of many Americans regarding the negative attributes of the Democratic Party. Most of these newly recruited and long-time conservatives with this new perception of Democrats will be loyal for decades to come.

Republicans can blame Trump

Donald J. Trump was elected without ever holding even a local political office. Therefore, it was objectively reasonable to expect him to make mistakes and have difficulty adjusting to the most difficult job in the world. The political party of the sitting President of the United States is expected to support him. During Trump's presidency, Republicans made a conscious effort to support Trump's policies, decisions, and President Trump in general. This resulted in Republicans making some uncharacteristic statements and decisions, some of which could not be adequately explained or justified. Based on Republicans being expected to support their President, they can always blame Trump if and when any of the decisions he made, or the laws he called for and they supported, do not produce the desired or promised outcome.

CHAPTER 4
Hypocrisy Only Exists In
The Minds Of Losers

Now, it is time for a blunt conversation. Life is about getting what you want. Conservative leaders understand that you must be willing to do whatever is necessary to get what you want. In fact, one of the keys to success in politics and life often involves either beating others to the punch, or convincing others that they should not act for some reason. Although the rationale that we give to others as to why they should not do something will be well thought out, have some basis in fact, and will be delivered with a straight face, we are only trying to keep the liberals from doing something we believe is against our conservative interests.

At some point liberals will learn that the rules are different for them. As conservatives, we cannot trust liberals to make sound decisions, or to do the right thing. As such, there are things that we can do that we will always advise liberals and Democrats not to do. We understand that this can be interpreted as "do as I say, not as I do." However, much like a parent that treats their child in this manner, conservatives have historically acted responsibly and therefore have earned the right to make the rules.

Getting our way, any way! That is what winners do…get their way. Liberals talk about doing things, but often fail to follow through just because someone voiced their opposition. Conservatives get shit done! Liberal opposition notwithstanding, if we believe that it fits within our conservative platform, we are still going to move forward. They will just have to learn to get over it. You will lose in life if you allow others to control what you think and do based upon what they think of your actions. Conservatives understand this and have remained at the forefront of determining morality and how others should act. As we rarely find a liberal's opinion valuable or to be backed by good morals, that a liberal may take offense to something that a conservative does or oppose is not of great import.

Hypocrisy should only be used to describe the actions of liberals and other non-conservatives. Conservatives have values and moral standards in fact, while liberals have espoused morals that they rarely live up to. As liberals have taken the position that society should accept everyone as they are instead of requiring all to conform to their behavior to comply with sound morals and values, it is up to us conservatives to assure that society continues to function based upon the appropriate values and principles. Consequently, conservative leaders must do everything necessary to keep the liberals in check. This sometimes will require that we make statements for the purpose of convincing liberals and others to do what will benefit the conservative cause. As the "greater good" is the driving force behind what conservatives are doing, that we may use "half-truths" or other somewhat deceptive means to accomplish our goal does not make our efforts immoral or hypocritical.

Conservatives are on a mission to save this country and make it better. Conservatives often see opportunity where others see obstacles. Healing and changing the direction of a country is not for the faint of heart. It takes a lot to fix the problems of a country as diverse and large as the United States. To conservatives, true hypocrisy would be claiming to be good people of high moral standards and not being willing to do whatever is necessary to help make this country better and successful. Conservatives are willing to accept the ridicule associated with doing the right thing.

As conservatives are typically good people with strong Christian values, we understand that some level of misunderstanding often accompanies those doing God's work. The important thing is to know that our goals align, and the result is the most important thing to pay attention to. I know you have heard that "God works in mysterious ways." Part of that mystery is how God uses people and events to implement His plan. You are not supposed to understand why everything happens, nor are you to question why. Remember, even the closest Disciples of Christ did not understand everything Jesus said and were described as lacking comprehension. Yet, they listened, followed Him, did what they were told, and were rewarded. Similarly, conservatives have learned that it is not necessary to understand every act taken as long as our goals align, and the results remain satisfactory. Do not let liberals block your blessings with their lies. Continue to follow God's plan as orchestrated by God-fearing conservatives.

At some point the citizens of this great nation had to step up and do what was necessary to save us all. As liberal leaders refused to, conservatives were forced to take control. Years of compromising our values to work with liberal administrations on the state and national level has left us with a country that we no longer recognize. Unfortunately, the current state of this nation evidences the fact that giving Democrats an inch virtually always results in them taking a mile or more. They are incapable of accepting what is fair. Their ultimate goals are always well beyond what they initially seek. To them, it matters not who made the pie, they do not want a piece of the pie; they want most of it so they can redistribute it to whomever they see fit. Conservatives are always omitted from the list of those slated to receive some of the pie stolen by Democrats.

These liberal Democrats are opportunist and attack our rights most often when Americans are distracted by some type of tragedy or unfortunate occurrence. For example, every time there is some type of shooting, especially those with multiple or minor victims, liberals waste no time campaigning against gun rights and introducing some unnecessary law to further restrict our right to bear arms as guaranteed by the United States Constitution. Instead of allowing the families of the victims to grieve, liberals take advantage of them and use them to further their political agenda. They do not respect the dead or these families. Democrats often accuse conservatives of being opportunistic and taking advantage of people. First, having situational awareness and appropriately reacting thereto is different from parading grieving family members in public and using their dead loved one's name for political gain. Next, how can Democrats claim that Republicans and conservatives are hypocrites when their hypocrisy is readily on display for anyone willing to pay attention? As Democrats lack the credibility to complain about a practice they routinely use, conservatives have no reason to worry about their claims of hypocrisy.

Speaking of hypocrisy, why is it that the Democrats always accuse Republicans of creating legislation harmful to African Americans when they have passed some of the most detrimental legislation to the advancement of African Americans? As Democrats are responsible for the Clinton Crime Bill, and the original aid to dependent children welfare program, they have little room to point fingers. Both pieces of legislation have been extremely detrimental to the progress of African Americans. To the extent that Democrats argue that there were unintended consequences, Democratic leaders should have known better and are responsible for researching and contemplating the possible and probable outcomes associated with the legislation they propose.

CHAPTER 5
Conservative Supreme Court Justices Are Valuable

Some may view mentioning the opportunities associated with the death of U.S. Supreme Court Justice Ruth Bader Ginsburg as being in bad taste. However, negative opinions about stating the obvious will not change the fact that Justice Ginsburg's death during the term of a Republican President could be used to further the conservative agenda in many ways. In fact, Justice Ginsburg's death left the Court with but three liberal Justices. Although one or more of the five conservative leaning justices have been known to side with the liberal justices on occasion, confirming a staunch conservative justice will virtually assure that our Republican conservative values will guide the rulings of the Supreme Court and the path of this great country for decades to come.

The importance of maintaining a conservative majority on the Supreme Court cannot be discounted. Every decision of the Supreme Court produces winners and losers, donors and recipients, beneficiaries and benefactors. That is, with each of the Court's decisions, some will benefit, whether indirectly, or directly. Some will be negatively affected by the decision, and others may never knowingly be affected by a decision. As virtually every Supreme Court decision based on a liberal majority has been at the expense of conservative donors and benefactors, confirming conservative Supreme Court Justices is imperative. To be clear, our goal must be to maintain our conservative values by reshaping America through the decisions handed down by a conservative Supreme Court.

Preventing then President Obama from filling Justice Scalia's seat on the Supreme Court was one of the best political moves by the Republican Party in the last 50 years. Although Republicans showed great strength and solidarity throughout Obama's presidency, remaining steadfast against allowing Merrick Garland's nomination to move forward was a great display of conviction and commitment to Republican values and principles. Public opinion notwithstanding, it was the right thing to do. The confirmation of Garland would have caused an ideological shift away from conservative values.

Throughout history, Democrats and liberals have used Congress to change the number of Supreme Court Justices for the purpose of maintaining "control" of the Supreme Court. That is, they have amended the Constitution to either reduce or increase the number of justices so that the number of justices that share their ideology maintains a majority. For example, from 1807 to 1837, the Supreme Court was comprised of seven justices. However, in 1837, Congress added two additional positions to the Supreme Court, which provided the Democratic president an opportunity to appoint two justices. By naming two additional justices that shared the party's political ideology, the direction of the Court was altered. Specifically, decisions made thereafter leaned more towards what the Democratic Party desired.

During the Civil War, the Supreme Court was increased to ten justices. This was important because it allowed the Union to maintain a majority on the Court. You see, there were a few key issues that separated the Confederacy from the Union. Now, had the Supreme Court determined that something done by the Union was unconstitutional and it related to any of these issues, a compromise may have been reached due to the Union's inability to maintain their position on that subject matter. Can you imagine the differences in the direction of this country had the causes of the Civil War been erased by a Supreme Court decision? Things would be quite different. Many lives would have been spared and a great deal of wealth would have survived the war, to be passed down for many generations. Additionally, those compromises would have resulted in a much stronger United States. Other countries would have been forced to follow our lead or risk being left behind. America would have expanded much faster, and the country would have received more respect from other nations.

In 1866, the Republicans controlled Congress and passed legislation reducing the Supreme Court to seven justices. In 1869, an act was passed that increased the number of justices to nine, where it has remained since that day. However, Democrats are at it again… trying to increase the number of justices because they cannot get their way. Like you, I have been waiting for Democrats to stop whining and complaining about not getting their way. Will they ever stop complaining? I wouldn't hold my breath. Democrats want to forward their agenda to continue damaging this country. The cry-baby Democrats believe that we stole their seat on the Court in 2016 and refuse to stop whining about it. If they had their way, Merrick Garland would be on the Supreme Court instead of the Attorney General. That seat belongs to Justice Neil Gorsuch, so get over it! Proposals for changing the Court have varied. While some favor term limits, many require an increase in the number of justices.

Democrats continue to take away rights from the hard-working men and women of America to promote confusion and transfer power to the liberal gender and sex-obsessed alphabet groups. As they keep expanding the types of people and behaviors they represent, which includes regularly adding more letters of the alphabet to their constituency, I will just refer to them as the alphabet folk. Based on their efforts to grow their constituency, I would not be surprised if all the letters of the alphabet eventually are utilized to represent one of the groups included in their constituency. Conservatives must do everything to block Democrats from expanding the Court... at least until the last year of Biden's presidency when we will have the ability to prevent him from moving forward with confirmation hearings.

Republicans nominated and confirmed every justice voted on during the time a Republican has been in the White House. The requests by Democrats for prolonged debates and investigations into the credentials and background of candidates nominated by President Trump were but attempts to stall. As Neil Gorsuch, Brett Kavanaugh, and Amy Coney Barrett were already members of the federal judiciary who had been previously confirmed by the Senate to be United States Circuit Court judges, all the theatrics by Democrats were unnecessary. The circus Democrats created surrounding the confirmation hearings was purposeful. Hopefully, the American people recognized it for the desperation tactics they were. To be clear, each of the candidates nominated by President Trump had already had their history and qualifications thoroughly investigated when they were nominated and subsequently confirmed to sit on a lower court. There should be no difference in the way their history and credentials are investigated for a seat on any federal court. And, if any outstanding issues were discovered during their initial investigations, they were surely explored to the extent required. That Democrats expected a second bite at the apple to delay or prevent the confirmation of any of three is shameful.

Conservatives must not miss another opportunity to shape the future of this country again. Having many of the justices be considered theoretically conservative is not enough. As all justices are free to change their mind and have been known to vote in a manner that does not align with our political ideology, our goal must be to only have justices on the Court that have a proven record of following conservative values. Moreover, they must not be afraid of any ridicule that they receive associated with their decisions and steadfast commitment to their conservative values that is forever present in their voting on cases and the opinions they author.

Let us explore just a few things that conservatives can prevent and accomplish by maintaining a supermajority of justices on the Supreme Court. First, as the Court determines the meaning and constitutionality of statutes and the rights provided to citizens by laws and the constitution, having a conservative court will help assure that conservative values will guide the Court's decisions on these critical issues. It can also prevent liberal justices from issuing majority opinions misinterpreting laws and the constitution. Preventing errors in judgment by liberals is extremely important.

Conservative Justices can correct previous errors by the Court

Conservatives have been at odds with the reasoning used by the Supreme Court majority to uphold abortion rights for decades. Previous Supreme Court decisions have held that the Due Process Clause protects "those rights guaranteed by the first eight Amendments of the Constitution and those rights deemed fundamental that are not mentioned anywhere in the Constitution." The problem is that the landmark case of *Roe v. Wade* found that the right to an abortion was based on the constitutional right to privacy derived from our right to "liberty" that is protected by the Fourteenth Amendment's Due Process Clause. As the Due Process Clause protects only those rights "deeply rooted in [American history] and tradition" and those essential to this country's "scheme of ordered liberty," the Court must examine abortion in this context. Several conservative Justices viewed *Roe* and the subsequent decisions confirming the constitutional right to abortion as not being ground in the Constitution and incorrectly decided due to the Justices in the majority being reluctant to go against stare decisis, which is the legal term for current Court precedent.

Fortunately, in 2022 Conservatives now outnumber the liberal Justices six to three. *Dobbs v. Jackson* was decided this year and the constitutional right to an abortion is no more. The authority to determine the abortion issue was returned to the individual states. In overturning *Roe*, the conservative Justices explained how the Court previously erred when deciding *Roe* and its progeny. Notably, Justice Thomas wrote a separate opinion that suggested that the Court review other substantive Due Process Clause precedent cases. As such, as long as Republicans work to bring cases in front of the U.S. Supreme Court that could result in changes to the laws that support conservative morals and values, we can utilize the Court to make the positive changes that we need in this country.

There are countless conservative attorneys and judges throughout the country. Conservatives are working in state, local, and federal government offices. Additionally, conservatives have a network of think tanks that provide guidance and support to law makers and business owners. Unlike Democrats, conservatives generally support other conservatives as we share common morals, goals and beliefs that are not a constant moving target due to the recruitment of random groups with their own agendas. This is the time for conservatives to effect change. As such, anyone with conservative values should join the party and take part in shaping the future.

CHAPTER 6
Winning The Republican Way

Generally, you need to get more votes than your opponent to win an election. That is, unless you are talking about a presidential election. Then, you just need to get more votes in states that result in your party obtaining the required 270 of the 538 electoral votes to become President. Although both the Democrats and Republicans have core groups of voters that they count on to support them in elections, Conservative voters are much more loyal to the Republican Party than the many groups that typically vote for Democratic candidates. While African Americans and liberal Whites make up the majority of the core voters Democrats count on for support, they often require motivation to go out and vote in elections.

Having more registered voters only counts if they vote

In this country, approximately five percent more Americans are registered to vote as Democrats than Republicans. That creates an uphill battle for Republicans in places where Democratic voters greatly outnumber Republicans. However, having a majority only helps if those voters routinely get out and vote in elections. Republicans are constantly motivating their constituents and reminding them how important it is to vote in every election. Although Democrats try to motivate their voters, they often require more motivation than do Republican voters.

Republicans have done well by instilling a sense of pride in being associated with the party and identifying as conservative. Instilling that sense of pride in self-identifying as a conservative has resulted in creating very loyal voters that often believe that voting and otherwise supporting the party is a responsibility that they dare not take lightly. Once something becomes a part of a person's identity, they generally are protective of their identity and will do whatever it takes to maintain it. Voting for the conservative candidate in an election is viewed as a duty to many people that have chosen to self-identify as conservative. It is more than just voting; supporting the conservative candidate has become part of the maintenance of one's sense of self.

Conversely, as Democrats often vary ideologically and often are not as committed to a strict view on issues, most Democrats have not adopted the same level of pride in their party as it is not a part of their overall identity. They do not have the strong sense of duty or responsibility to vote for the liberal candidate that Republicans have when a conservative candidate is on the ballot. That lack of connection has resulted in Democrats being more prone to party defection and failing to go out and vote.

Too many cooks spoil the soup

Republicans have had consistent views on the issues the party finds important and rarely change their position on an issue to appease newcomers to the party. Generally, if you are switching to the Republican Party, you either must adopt the expressed conservative morals, goals, and ideology, or you will end up being disappointed because the party will not change for you. Republicans are transparent with their expectations. While Republicans will try to convince voters that they should adopt conservative values and goals, they are not in the habit of changing their direction to suit others.

Democrats are different. The Democratic Party appears to be in a perpetual search for new voters with special interests. It seems like the Democrats cannot meet a special interest group that they are not willing to promise to help…if they would just support the Democratic Party by voting for them. Importantly, I stated, "promise to help," and not in fact help. Democrats have so many special interest groups now that they no longer have a well-defined ideology due to impossibility. Virtually every group registered as a Democrat has multiple interests within the group itself, resulting in a myriad of morals, beliefs, goals, and interests. There is no uniformity of thought. There are too many groups jockeying for position and attention from party leaders.

You are smart, a good person, and will be rich

Republicans win because they check all the important personhood boxes. First, the decision to become a Republican is a very smart choice. If you put in the work and make your needs known, you can benefit from your affiliation to the party. You made your vote count and were not swayed by guilt or empty promises. Importantly, you are smart because you are no longer allowing yourself to be controlled by a bunch of people that just want to use you for free.

Next, Republicans possess the honesty, generosity, humility, morality, work ethic, kindness, and other attributes of a "good person." As the Democrats include more and more groups that lack traditional morals, they continue to drift away from the standards necessary for many to view them as good people. Specifically, as Democrats continue to cater, support, and condone the actions of those with alternative lifestyles, the more people will defect from the party because of such.

Finally, if followed for long enough, Republican values and ideology will result in the person following becoming rich. Republicans generally believe in encouraging capitalism, limited taxation, quality public education, a limited federal government, but strong local government, freedom, and significant financial investment for the future. Following the values and goals of Republicans results in a person working hard to achieve, not wasting money, saving money, investing money, making important contacts that can help you achieve your goals, and associating with other like-minded individuals. The immersion in this type of culture is greatly beneficial to your financial health. In fact, even someone that begins their life poor can achieve riches or wealth if they join the Republican Party and strictly follow the aforementioned. Although it may take longer, by watching their spending, saving, investing, and taking advantage of the available contacts within the party, even someone that began life working in fast food or retail can move up classes and eventually become rich and retire early. It just takes discipline.

As being a Republican provides you with the three things that most people desire, why would anyone want to belong to a different party? The Democrats continue to provide voters with reasons why they should be Republican. Being a Republican just makes life better. Who doesn't desire a better life? If you are able to find someone, they are likely already a Republican.

AFTERWORD

This book is the culmination of over thirty years of being a registered voter, discussing politics with people of many different races, religions, ages, and political ideology, earning multiple advanced degrees, including a law degree, and researching the subject-matter. After much thought it has become apparent that Democrats just do not understand what people want and more importantly, they do not understand what voters are willing to accept. While Republicans have focused on the same few issues for decades, Democrats continue to invite new special interest groups to their party resulting in new issues for the party to address. Republicans wisely invite others to join the party and adopt the values, beliefs, and goals currently shared within the party.

Many Latino and African Americans that have worked hard to become successful business owners and those that have successfully climbed the corporate ladder no longer feel as though they have a place within the Democratic Party. Moreover, they may feel as though they no longer have a great deal in common with people that look like them but have not been equally as successful. Their increase in income and status often results in a change in their needs, desires, and concerns. It also usually results in them moving into a "better" neighborhood with neighbors that may be more diverse, or of a different race. However, their new neighbors will generally be within the same socioeconomic class as they are. By interacting with their new neighbors, they discover how much they have in common and that their new status and surroundings have caused a shift in their concerns, how they are treated, and in some cases, many of the issues associated with being a member of their minority group no longer affects them in the same manner, if at all.

Successful Black people often feel forced to move due to what they explain as mistreatment of those in their community that is at least partially due to jealousy. They often experience hostility within their community, the loss of old friends, and in some cases vandalism or theft of their property. They often hear whispers within the community that they are no longer Black because they have made certain changes, or that they must think that they are better than the other Blacks in the community because of their success, or the addition of material things that others within the community cannot afford. This often drives them out of their community and into a new one where they will be accepted.

Successful Latinos can have similar experiences within their communities. Changes to their income, status, or success, often rubs some within their community the wrong way. They may hear people within their community stating that they act as if they are White, or that they are no longer Spanish enough. Similarly, some successful Latinos move to new communities where they feel welcome and are surrounded by others with things in common.

While successful Blacks and Latinos are shunned by some members of their race and communities, they still face some of the same issues and negative stereotypes that may be associated with their race. That is, they still feel as though they must think about or always recognize their race or ethnicity. After working so hard to achieve, most just want a break from having to think about it. They just want to be a normal person like everyone else. Just for a moment, they do not want to be viewed as Black or Latino. It's not that they do not know who they are, or are in any way ashamed of their heritage, they need a break from being recognized as different and everything that goes along with it. Why can't he just be seen as a man, or she as a woman? Why can't they solely focus on living life instead of having to live as a _________ American?

Democrats fail to address the new concerns, issues, and needs of successful Blacks and Latinos. Instead, they expect successful Black people and Latinos to go along with the same old song and dance while they get nothing from their affiliation to the party. In fact, they are expected to contribute more due to their success. Any objections are often met with claims that they are letting their fellow Blacks or Latinos down by not consenting to whatever is asked of them. Republicans accept them into the party as just another member of the party, not a representative of their race or culture. As conservative ideology focuses on the party's core values, goals, and issues, and not issues associated with minority groups, Blacks and Latino conservatives get that much needed break and can participate as just another member of the party. They no longer must contribute more based on their race. Importantly, they get something from being a Republican. Unlike the Democrats that will discuss a request for action made by a constituent for years without taking any action, Republicans will get right on a request, produce a solution, and implement it. While Democrats discuss if something can be done, Republicans get things done, then subsequently discuss how successful the things they have done were.

Ultimately, the Democrats are losing voters because they have too many distinct groups with different agendas to fully satisfy any of these groups. How could they ever expect to satisfy so many groups, some with conflicting interests? Just how do those within the "faith and family left," considered to be socially conservative, reconcile their beliefs to allow them to support same-sex marriage, abortion, or any of the alternative lifestyles now supported by the Democrats? How do the economically moderates and the progressives both get what they want? Every group wants equality and a piece of the pie that Democrats have already promised to a different group. The Democrats have turned into a party of people looking to feel good about themselves because they claim to be working on so many causes. The problem for Democrats is that they get little done, and what they do accomplish, except for giving away money, is often written, or otherwise done in a manner that can be corrected by Republicans without a great deal of effort once back in office.

SOURCES AND REFERENCES

annualreviews.org, Valelly, Richard M., *LGBT Politics and American Political Development*, (Mar. 8, 2012), https://www.annualreviews.org/doi/pdf/10.1146/annurev-polisci-061709-104806 (last visited 10/31/2022).

apnews.com, Articles, Gresko, Jessica, *Supreme Court expands gun rights, with nation divided*, (Jun. 23, 2022), https://apnews.com/article/supreme-court-guns-decision-58d01ef8bd48e816d5f8761ffa84e3e8 (last visited 10/31/2022).

bbc.com, News, Horton, Jake, *George Floyd: How far have African Americans come since the 1960s*, (May 24, 2021), https://www.bbc.com/news/world-us-canada-52992795 (last visited 10/31/2022).

brookings.edu, Hochschild, Jennifer L., *American Racial and Ethnic Politics in the 21ˢᵗ Century: A cautious look ahead*, (Mar. 1, 1998), https://www.brookings.edu/articles/american-racial-and-ethnic-politics-in-the-21st-century-a-cautious-look-ahead/ (last visited 10/31/2022).

businessinsider.com, Business Insider, Lebowitz, Shana, *11 common traits of highly intelligent people*, (Apr. 19, 2019), https://www.businessinsider.com/8-common-traits-of-highly-intelligent-people-2016-7 (last visited 11/1/2022).

civilrights.org, Podcast, The Leadership Conference on Civil and Human Rights, Gonzalez, Vanessa N., Scott, Bobby, Rep., *Vision For Justice: The '94 Crime Bill*, (Jul. 13, 2021), https://civilrights.org/podcast/visionforjustice-e2/# (last visited 11/3/2022).

constitution.congress.gov, Constitution of the United States, *Second Amendment*,
https://constitution.congress.gov/constitution/amendment-2/ (last visited 10/31/2022).

crf-usa.org, Constitutional Rights Foundation, *BRIA 14 3 a How Welfare Began in the United States*, https://www.crf-usa.org/bill-of-rights-in-action/bria-14-3-a-how-welfare-began-in-the-united-states.html (last visited 10/31/2022).

democrats.org, Who-We-Are, LGBTQ Community, https://democrats.org/who-we-are/who-we-serve/lgbtq-community/ (last visited 11/1/2022).

drivethru.com, Drive Thru Team, *Feeling Intelligent: A Guide To Your Emotions*, (May 8, 2021), https://divethru.com/feeling-intelligent-a-guide-to-your-emotions/ (last visited 11/1/2022).

econlib.org, Brown, Tarnell, *A Brief Look at Why Prohibition Laws Don't Work*, (August 26, 2020) https://www.econlib.org/a-brief-look-at-why-prohibition-laws-dont-work/ (last visited 10/31/2022).

goodrx.com, LGBTQ+ Health, Le, Kevin PharmD, *What Does the Full LGBTQIA+ Acronym Stand For*, (Oct. 19, 2022), https://www.goodrx.com/health-topic/lgbtq/meaning-of-lgbtqia (last visited 10/31/2022).

history.com, News, Pilon, Mary, *How Bill Clinton's Welfare Reform Changed America*, (Aug. 29, 2018), https://www.history.com/news/clinton-1990s-welfare-reform-facts (last visited 10/30/2022).

hopesandfears.com, Mashurova, Nina, *Why do people want to be good*, http://www.hopesandfears.com/hopes/now/question/216881-why-do-people-want-to-be-good (last visited 11/1/2022).

investopedia.com, Taxes, Floyd, David, *Explaining the Trump Tax Reform Plan*, (Apr. 30, 2022), https://www.investopedia.com/taxes/trumps-tax-reform-plan-explained/ (last visited 10/31/2022).

jec.senate.gov, American Enterprise Institute, *America's Invisible Felon Population: A Blind Spot in US National Statistics*, Eberstadt, Nicholas, PhD, (May 22, 2019), https://www.jec.senate.gov/public/_cache/files/b23fea23-8e98-4bcd-aeed-edcc061a4bc0/testimony-eberstadt-final.pdf (last visited 10/31/2022).

law.jrank.org, *Man-in-the-House Rule*, https://law.jrank.org/pages/8412/Man-in-House-Rule.html (last visited 10/30/2022).

mikejohnson.house.gov, U.S. Congressman Mike Johnson, *7 Core Principles of Conservatism*, https://mikejohnson.house.gov/7-core-principles-of-conservatism/ (last visited 11/1/2022).

nmaahc.si.edu, *A Changing America: 1968 and BEYOND*, https://nmaahc.si.edu/explore/exhibitions/changing-america (last visited 10/31/2022).

news.bloombergtax.com, Daily Tax Report, O'Neal, Lydia, *The Trump Tax Cust: Promises Made, Promises Kept*, (Jan. 26, 2021), https://news.bloombergtax.com/daily-tax-report/the-trump-tax-cuts-promises-made-promises-kept-1 (last visited 11/2/2022).

penntoday.upenn.edu, *Unpacking Latino conservatism, https://penntoday.upenn.edu/news/unpacking-latino-conservatism* (last visited 10/31/2022).

pewresearch.org, Pew Research Center, Desilver, Drew, *A closer look at who identifies as Democrat and Republican*, (July 1, 2014), https://www.pewresearch.org/fact-tank/2014/07/01/a-closer-look-at-who-identifies-as-democrat-and-republican/ (last visited 10/31/2022).

pewresearch.org, Pew Research Center, Krogstad, Jens Manuel; Edwards, Khadijah, and Lopez, Mark Hugo, *Hispanics' views on key issues facing the nation*, (Sept. 29, 2022), https://www.pewresearch.org/race-ethnicity/2022/09/29/hispanics-views-on-key-issues-facing-the-nation/ (last visited 10/31/2022).

pewresearch.org, Pew Research Center, *Progressive Left*, (Nov. 9, 2021), https://www.pewresearch.org/politics/2021/11/09/progressive -left/ (last visited 11/1/2022).

poorpeoplescampaign.org, Reports, *Unleashing the Power of Poor and Low-Income Americans*, (Aug. 11, 2020), https://www.poorpeoplescampaign.org/resource/power-of-poor-voters/ (last visited 10/31/2022).

projects.fivethirtyeight.com, Best, Ryan; Radcliffe, Mary, and Rogers, Kaleigh, *Just How Far Apart Are The Two Parties On Gun Control*, (June 7, 2022), https://projects.fivethirtyeight.com/gun-control-polling-2022/ (last visited 10/31/2022).

psychologytoday.com, Bredehoft, David J. Ph.D., *All They Want To Be Is Rich, Famous, and Good Looking*, (Jan. 11, 2019), https://www.psychologytoday.com/us/blog/the-age-overindulgence/201901/all-they-want-be-is-rich-famous-and-good-looking (last visited 11/1/2022).

psychologytoday.com, Ocklenburg, Sebastian, Ph.D., *Is There a Connection Between Being Smart and Being Liked*, (Apr. 2, 2021), https://www.psychologytoday.com/us/blog/the-asymmetric-brain/202104/is-there-connection-between-being-smart-and-being-liked (last visited 11/1/2022).

psychologytoday.com, Samuel, Lawrence R., Ph.D., *The Psychology of Wealth*, (Dec. 5, 2015), https://www.psychologytoday.com/us/blog/psychology-yesterday/201512/the-psychology-wealth (last visited 11/1/2022).

supremecourt.gov, Opinions, *D.C. v. Heller*, https://www.supremecourt.gov/opinions/07pdf/07-290.pdf (last visited 10/31/2022).

supremecourt.gov, Opinions, *Dobbs v. Jackson*,
https://www.supremecourt.gov/opinions/21pdf/19-
1392_6j37.pdf (last visited 10/31/2022).

supreme.justia.com, Justia, Cases, *Roe v. Wade*, 410 U.S. 113 (1973),
https://supreme.justia.com/cases/federal/us/410/113/ (last
visited 10/31/2022).

theatlantic.com, Politics, Friedersdorf, Conor, *What Americans Mean
When They Say They're Conservative*, (Jan. 27, 2012),
https://www.theatlantic.com/politics/archive/2012/01/what-
americans-mean-when-they-say-theyre-conservative/252099/
(last visited 11/1/2022).

U.S. Const. amend. II.

U.S. Const. amend. I.

U.S. v. Miller, 307 U.S. 174 (1939).

williamsinstitute.law.ucla.edu, Meyer, Ilan H., Choi, Soon Kyu,
*Differences Between LGB Democrats and Republicans in Identity and
Community Connectedness*, (Oct. 2020),
https://williamsinstitute.law.ucla.edu/publications/lgb-party-
affiliation/ (last visited 11/1/2022).

* The many people of different gender, races, ages, religions, political
affiliations, and lifestyles that I spoke with throughout the years.

ABOUT THE AUTHOR

P. S. Mann has a Master of Business Administration (MBA) and a Juris Doctorate (J.D.). He also is a former federal judicial law clerk to a Senior United States District Court Judge. He is a business owner, and he advises business owners.